The Art of Meditating with Cats

Dawn Allen

Copyright © 2020 by Dawn Allen
Written and Illustrated by Dawn Allen
Edited by Keala / Constance Lehmann

ISBN-13: 978-0-9816571-6-5
ISBN-10: 0-9816571-6-8
Dawn Allen: dawnallen.net
Dawn's Animal Connection: dawnallen.org
Westfield, MA

Table of Contents

Meditating with Cats

Cats have many gifts to offer us, and meditation with your cat is a wonderful way to open your heart to receive their teachings. Connecting with their love, wisdom, whimsy, charm, and more, for even a few minutes a day, can enrich your life.

Meditating with your cat is also an opportunity to send focused messages to your cat to help them better understand you. You will be able to let them know how you feel and what your intentions are in a way in which they can really "hear" you. Your cat will most likely love meditating with you!

In general, meditation is about contemplation and reflection for various purposes, such as emotional calm or spiritual awareness. For each meditation in this book, I let you know what the focus or purpose is for that particular exercise, but consider it a launching-off point; your cat may guide you in other directions.

The goal of most meditations is to bring your mind and body into a state of relaxation—to feel emotionally calm and centered and to be focused in the moment (letting go of thoughts of the past and future). Cats make great teachers for meditation because they easily achieve a state similar to what I have just described. Most people find it easiest to meditate while sitting or lying comfortably in silence or with soft music in the background. Closing your eyes will help eliminate distractions and allow you to focus inward. Becoming aware of your breath can also help focus your mind and reduce distractions.

The quality of your meditation and your cat's experience is not conditioned on how much time you spend meditating. The length of your meditation depends on how you feel and your goals. Maybe you need only two minutes of relaxation with your cat before work, or maybe you need 45 minutes of calm contemplation. Your cat might leave the meditation; you may choose to continue or quit when they walk away.

Each meditation that follows comes with specific instructions. Read the "human" instructions to yourself and then read the "cat" instructions aloud to your cat (unless your cat can read). Most importantly, go with the flow and follow your cat's lead. Remember, it is not possible for your cat to distract your meditation when, in fact, they are leading your meditation.

In the Moment Meditation

The purpose of this meditation is to experience being in the moment with your cat.

Cats live their whole lives in the here and now. Being in the moment is normal life to cats; and while they have many lessons to teach us, that is their core curriculum. When your mind is running in too many directions, take the time to settle in with your cat and try this meditation.

Humans
Sit or lie down in the same room as your cat; they don't need to be right next to you. Close your eyes and allow your cat to guide you on how to be present to this moment. Gently let the past and future melt away as you learn from your furry meditation master.

Cats
Help your human focus on the here and now. You know your person best; help them in whatever way seems most appropriate. You are free to leave at any time.

Gratitude Meditation

The purpose of this meditation is to tune in to gratitude (which can help us humans have more inner peace) and to offer our cats gratitude because they deserve it!

Cats aren't famous for showing gratitude, but they should be—cats really do appreciate their homes, even though they might not seem to show it. Cats can be perceived as bossy rather than grateful because they are really good at demanding what they want. Their gratitude is implied. (Another lesson you can learn from your cat: ask for what you really want.)

Humans
Snuggle with your cat (or nearby) and feel relaxed, allowing your mind to drift from thought to thought. Begin to focus on thoughts and feelings of gratitude. You don't need to linger on any thoughts or search for thoughts, just allow gratitude to gently flow through your mind. Silently send your cat gratitude for everything they give to you. When you are ready, allow your mind to become still and imagine what thoughts of gratitude your cat has.

Cats
Hang out with your person if you want. Relish in their gratitude. Share your thoughts on what makes you most grateful.

Love Meditation

The purpose of this meditation is to tell your cat that you love them. You probably already communicate "I love you" all the time in all kinds of noisy human ways, such as hugs and kisses and songs and nicknames. This is something a little more quiet and subtle; your cat might appreciate it.

We all want our cats to know how much we love them. Sometimes we worry that maybe they don't understand when we take them to the vet or clip their nails. It can be nice to offer this reassurance. Also, sending love can open us in surprising ways to receive love back.

Humans
Close your eyes and hold your cat's image in your mind's eye. Feel your heart open and your love for them pour out. Be in the moment, allowing thoughts to fade away and your love for your cat to take over. When you are ready, gently quiet your mind and emotions. Be open to your cat's love. Be receptive.

Cats
Be your loving little self!

Purr Meditation

Experiencing a cat's purr against your body might be one of the most magical moments in life. The purpose of this meditation is to fully enjoy your cat's purr.

Humans
This meditation will be initiated by your cat when the moment is right for them—if you are busy, you must stop immediately! Let your cat snuggle with you or settle nearby and start purring. Close your eyes and allow your thoughts to drift away. Immerse yourself in the vibration of the purr. Enjoy. Cherish the moment.

Cats
As often as you like, share your purr with your human. Feel free to choose a time that appears to be the least convenient for your human friend. How important can their computer be, right?

Going Away Meditation

The purpose of this meditation is to prepare your cat for you being away from home (on a trip).

Before you go away, you can meditate with your cat. I find that this meditation significantly helps reduce the stress of being away.

Humans

Start with a quiet meditation, sending love. Then think simple thoughts and images about what your cat can expect while you are away. Visualize the nights one by one, count them out up to five. (If your trip is more than five nights, let them know you will be gone for a while.) Sit quietly after the explanation, allowing your mind to be still. Lovingly wait to see whether your cat has a response. It is okay if you don't know whether they are responding, it is still polite to listen. While you are away you can practice "Love Meditation" (page 11), from a distance.

Cats

You might not like the situation, but please take into consideration what your person is telling you; it could help you while they are gone.

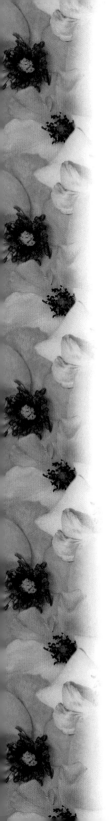

Cat Wisdom Meditation

Cats have a life perspective that is different from ours. Their views on the meaning of life, spirituality, and so many other topics can be enlightening for us humans. The purpose of this meditation is to explore viewing life like a cat.

Humans

Close your eyes and sit comfortably with or near your cat. Allow yourself to notice sounds, smells, and textures around you. As thoughts come into your mind, relax; you don't need to fully empty your mind. As you relax and feel present in the moment, allow yourself to receive your cat's wisdom in whatever form it takes, such as thoughts, visions, emotions, etc.

Cats

Your person's mind is open to whatever advice or wisdom you have for them. If your person relaxes, I hope you will share your thoughts and energy with them … or sit on your person in that awkward way that we both know isn't really comfortable—that usually gets their attention.

Meditation on Health

Maybe your cat doesn't feel well or has discomfort. It can be hard to tell. This meditation won't be the same as a vet visit, but it can be helpful to try to be in tune with your cat and how they are feeling.

Humans
Find a really quiet, relaxed time in the house. It is best to clear all distractions for this meditation.

Start by tuning into your own body and take note of any sensations of discomfort. You don't need to clear any of your sensations, just take note of how you feel.

Next, silently invite your cat to show you how they feel. Relax and allow yourself to notice any sensations in your body that are new or different.

At the end of the meditation, let go of any new sensations in your body and go back to being fully yourself without holding onto any of your cat's symptoms.

Cats
Let your person know how you feel. No need to be stoic today, let them know your full truth.

Well-Being Meditation for Cats

When cats aren't feeling well, your quiet, attentive, non-invasive presence can feel very comforting to them.

Humans

Begin by centering your own energy. Slow your breathing and become very calm and grounded. Offer to send healing energy to your cat. Gently focus on uplifting your cat and visualize them feeling well. Hold your cat in your mind's eye, filling them with love and wellness.

Cats

Make yourself comfortable. Settle in wherever you feel best. When you feel you have received enough energy, you can tune out your person or leave.

Healing Meditation for Humans

The purpose of this meditation is to accept the healing your cat is offering you.

When you aren't feeling well physically or emotionally, your cat often knows and wants to help. Their loving presence and warm bodies can be very healing. The healing may benefit your emotional or physical health, or both.

Humans

If you have an amenable cat, you can gently ask them to do the healing meditation with you; otherwise, this meditation will be initiated by your cat. If your cat approaches, offering healing, all you need to do is drop everything—even your phone! Close your eyes, let go of any expectations of how you should feel, and accept your cat's loving healing energy.

Cats

Thank you for being so sweet and caring.

Feel Like a Feline Meditation

In this meditation, you will explore feeling like a cat. Your body might learn a lot!

Your cat looks so comfortable—whether stretched out, leaping, or balled up in a sunbeam. They are flexible and relaxed. They love their cat body!

Humans
In this meditation, try feeling like a cat! Close your eyes and imagine yourself in your cat's body. Notice how relaxed, agile, flexible, and warm you feel. Notice the differences and similarities of your bodies. Notice how your cat loves their body, free of judgments.

Cats
Just be yourself—you rock!

Feral Cat Meditation

The purpose of this meditation is to help feral or skittish cats feel safer with you.* By mindfully ignoring your skittish cat, you give them time to get accustomed to "safe" human energy. It is like giving your cat an invisibility cloak. After a few weeks they will get closer and closer to you.

Humans

Determine how to be near your cat but still have them feel safe. They might want to stay hidden and that is fine; you can do the meditation from across the room if that is what your cat prefers.

Focus your energy and thoughts on your own breathing. Stay present with your own feelings, and don't put any thoughts or energy toward your cat. Slowly notice each of your body parts from toes to head. Even if your cat chooses to approach, keep your eyes closed and continue to ignore their presence. Focus only on your own body and deep relaxation.

Cats

Do only what feels totally comfortable.

*If you have a skittish cat who is afraid of other people, try "Peace and Sanity Meditation" on page 34.

Playful Meditation

The purpose of this meditation is to help humans live in the moment and drop judgments as well as to fulfill your cat's need for strategic play. Often people stop dangling string for their cat when the cat stops running and leaping. Unfortunately, most mature cats love to sit very still and strategize how they might catch the string. When people judge them as "bored," no one wins.

Humans

This meditation involves keeping your eyes open and being active. Choose your cat's favorite toy. Clear your mind of daily thoughts and put all of your attention on playing with your cat. Be in the moment. Let go of any judgments. If you find yourself thinking that your cat is bored, take a deep breath and let the thought go. Appreciate your cat for whatever play style they may choose.

Commit to playing until your cat physically leaves, falls asleep, or permanently looks away from the toy. Even if they look "bored," if their eyes are on the toy, keep playing. Taking it all the way will be very special for them and is a great meditative practice in patience and living in the moment for you.

Cats

Do what you want. Today is your day to play, or not, whatever.

Uplifting Meditation

The purpose of this meditation is to let your cat elevate your mood.

Cats know how to feel good. Let your cat show you the way! Each cat has their own way of being uplifting. They may uplift you through play, mischief, peace, snuggles, etc.

Humans
Stop what you are doing and soak up whatever fun or peace your cat has in store for you right this minute. I call this "Paws for Cuteness." Watch them zoom around the house, or catch them having one of those adorable twitching dreams, or gaze at your relaxed cat in a sunbeam. Let all other distractions slip away.

Cats
Be yourself. (Humans try that, too.)

Spirit Cat Meditation

I don't know for sure what happens when our furry friends die. What I think is that they are still with us in some way, free yet still connected. The purpose of this meditation is to gently address your grief in whatever way is most healing for you.

Humans

This meditation works best for some people when they are in movement (a slow walk, raking leaves, etc.). Other people find it easier to focus in a more traditional eyes-closed resting meditation. You might want to try it both ways. Take this opportunity to first focus inward and allow yourself to process any feelings you have around your cat's passing, including any guilt, regret, or trauma.

When you are ready, relax and gently reach out to your cat, sending any thoughts you want them to know, things left unsaid before they died, and feelings of love or appreciation.

As your mind quiets, allow yourself to receive the love and presence of your spirit cat.

Spirit Cats

Thank you for being there for your human.
Cats (if you have a physical cat in the room)
Please help your human experience the messages from their spirit cat(s).

Peace and Sanity Meditation

The purpose of this meditation is to help your cat feel peaceful and safer. You can tailor the meditation to cover your cat's concerns; for example, construction in the house, a guest coming, or a new dog.

Humans
You can do this meditation with your cat nearby or in the next room. This is all about emotion, so close your eyes and get into a very calm, peaceful emotional state. Send reassuring thoughts to your cat about the situation as you allow yourself to feel more and more peaceful.

Cats
You're scared and stressed, and you have good reasons for your feelings. You might feel better and see things differently if you tune in to your human's reassurances.

Peace for Multiple Cats

This meditation is for cats who are not getting along. Do this meditation with one cat at a time.

Humans
Relax into a calm, deep meditation. Feel peaceful. Visualize harmony and peace between the cats. Show them emotionally what it would feel like to have peace between them.

Repeat this meditation with each cat every day. It is fine if you keep the meditation brief; just 3–5 minutes is plenty.

Cats
Remind your person to react peacefully even in the moments when fighting erupts.

Personal Space Meditation

Sometimes you want to hug or pet your cat, but maybe they don't want that. Instead of trying to change your cat's mind, let your cat teach you their boundaries.

Humans
In this meditation you will sit in the same room as your cat but not touching them. With your eyes open, softly focus out the window or across the room. Pay attention to the sounds around you. Allow your cat to show you how close they want to be. Your cat might want to sit nearby or appreciate you from across the room—either is fine. Maybe they will come and ask to be petted, but wait until you are sure they are really asking for touch before you take any action.

Cats
Do whatever you want. You're a fabulous cat!

Preparation Meditation

Cats can't think about the future. If you want to tell them about an upcoming event, such as a move or a vet visit, you can do that in this meditation. They won't understand you fully now, but when the event happens, they will have *déjà vu* and hopefully feel comforted by the sense that they now know what is happening. Do this meditation only a day or hours before the event.

Humans
Choose a time when your cat is quiet and not distracted. Sit very quietly and with a calm emotion visualize the upcoming event. Picture it like a movie running in your mind, happening exactly as it would in real life. Make sure you visualize your cat feeling calm and secure in the movie.

Cats
This might not make sense to you now, but pay attention anyway.

Changing a Behavior Meditation

The purpose of this meditation is to ask your cat for a specific behavior. This isn't a magic wand but can help you and your cat coexist better. Promise me that this isn't the first meditation in the book you try. Please meditate for several days with your cat before deploying this one.

Humans
Close your eyes and get in a very calm relaxed state. Tell your cat that you want to understand why they do what they do (claws on furniture, peeing on dog bed, etc.). Sit quietly and seek first to understand without judgment. Toward the end of the meditation, in a very peaceful emotional state, visualize what you want from your cat. The instructions must be stated in the positive, such as "Keep the house clean and pee only in your litterbox." It will not be effective if you are agitated or if you try to tell your cat what "not" to do.

Cats
Your person is going to do their best to understand you. Hopefully, you will also do your best to understand your human and correct whatever radical behavior is unacceptable to them. However, you do have free will, so prove it by glaring at your human whenever they make a mistake … or just because it's Tuesday.

Warmth and Love Meditation

Cats have a higher body temperature than humans, plus they have a permanent fur coat so they feel extra warm next to your skin. Next time your cat snuggles up to you, you can try this meditation.

Humans
Close your eyes and focus on your cat's warmth. Let all of your thoughts and distractions melt away as you focus on their warm furry body.

As you receive the warmth, imagine that the warmth is equivalent to love. Allow the love of your cat to envelop and fill you.

When you feel full of warmth and love, shine the warmth and love back to your cat. Let all your love for your cat flow out of you and picture them receiving it.

Cats
Snuggle up with your person if you want to feel extra toasty warm and loved today!

Deeper Understanding

The purpose of this meditation is to take a deep dive into understanding your cat's behavior and thinking. Choose something about your cat that you want to know more about. (For example, I might ask my cat Henry more about why he brings me a toy mouse while meowing loudly.)

Humans

Close your eyes and focus on relaxing your breathing. Imagine your cat's breath and your breath becoming synchronized. Slowly imagine sliding into your cat's perspective, seeing things through their eyes, hearing things through their ears. From this new level of connection, imagine a behavior that you are curious about. Imagine doing that behavior from this vantage point, inside your cat's perspective. See what you learn about your cat.

Cats

Help your human to see beyond your behavior and give them a sense of what it means to be a cat and who you really are. Show them your emotions. Surprise them!

Author and Artist Dawn Allen

My older brother was a cat. He was patient, loving, and grumpy. As a toddler I asked too much of him, but he always forgave me. I would refuse to go to bed without my cat, so he would fall asleep with me; but my parents later told me he would sneak out and hunt at night only to return to bed in the morning. My dad and I shared a passion for cats, and, after our first cat died, we went on to have three more before I went to college.

At Goddard College I studied "Holistic Methods of Working with Animals." After I graduated I started my practice as an Animal Communicator, which continues to be my job today, more than 20 years later.

Creating fiber art quilts has been another passion of mine since I was a teenager. Recently, I developed a new technique for combining digital art and fiber art. First I create the portraits of the cats on my computer, painting with a stylus pen instead of a traditional paintbrush. Then I get my artwork printed on cotton fabric and use a technique called "free-motion quilting" to draw all over the image with thread. (Lots and lots of thread!)

In 2019 I allowed myself to dive deep into my cat obsession. I came up with the concept for this book—a way to combine my love of talking about cats, connecting with cats, and depicting cats in my artwork.

Artist Website: dawnallen.net
Animal Communication Website: dawnallen.org

Appreciation

Thank you to the following photographers who shared their cat photos to be used as references for my artwork in this book.

Lyu Novozhilov, cover, 5 (center), 50
(photographer and breeder of cats; Hot Flame Lyumur, Lapushka Iz Tverskogo Knyazhestva and Alrisha Lymur)
Fallon Boze, 2
JBR83, 5 (left)
Jamie Butterworth Lord, 5 (right)
Connie Cochran, 6
A. H., 9
Nicole Baker, 10
Krista Carboni, 12
Christy Ann Elamma, 17
Jessica M., 19
Timothy Comeux, 21
Andi Balser, 22
Sam Qaissouni, 24
Yvon Roelands, 27
Sandra Lopes, 29
Leslie Nuttelman, 30
Andrea N., 32
Brittany Pessotti, 35
Lisa D., 36
Tara Hayes, 39
M. Bradshaw, 44
Connie Lipton, 46
Lois Uliana, 49

With much gratitude and appreciation, thank you to Keala; the best editor in the world!

Dawn Allen

Made in the USA
Middletown, DE
18 January 2021